Sophie

Praise for Sophie

Sophie Kamler's story sweeps up the history of the twentieth century in one life. From pogroms to displacement, from freedom's devouring ambitions to love that can endure years of suffering—this book of fragments, voices, memories and reflections offers readers gem after gem of wisdom. I found it unputdownable, almost holding my breath all the way through.

—Kevin Brophy

Here is a story of our times—of women in our times, of refugees and exiles in our times—elegantly told in intimate pieces through the life of Sophie Kamler, the author's grandmother. Sophie does what literature is supposed to do: it takes someone else's story and makes it your own.

—Mark Tredinnick

So much of who we are is predicated on the decisions, hardships, and downright luck of our ancestors. Barbara Kamler has written a deeply moving tribute to her grandmother Sophie in a series of vignettes that engage with the complexity and limitations of memoir, leaning into these connections, parallels and palimpsets to create a composite portrait that feels expansive and true.

—Magdalena Ball

Sophie
Barbara Kamler

Sophie
ISBN 978 1 76109 902 1
Copyright © Barbara Kamler 2024
Cover and internal design by Graham Davidson
Image: Author's own photograph of Sophie, dated 1938

First published 2024 by
Ginninderra Press
PO Box 2 Bentleigh 3204
www.ginninderrapress.com.au

*for those who have passed,
those who remain,
and those who will come after*

Contents

Author's Note — 9
   Preamble — 9
   Resources for writing — 13
   More than words — 15
   A partial family tree — 17

I Departure — 19
   Fleeing Płońsk (1907) — 19
   Płońsk dismantled — 22
   Płońsk revisited (1973) — 24

II Arrival — 27
   Sophie finds work — 27
   Friends for life (circa 1908) — 31
   Abe finds Sophie — 33

III Marriage — 37
   Partners for life (circa 1911) — 37
   Wedding day — 39
   No children — 41

IV Motherhood — 43
   Sophie and her kids (circa 1920) — 43
   The best mother — 45
   The eldest son — 46
   The only daughter — 48
   Tough love — 50

V Business — 53
   The gangsters came — 53
   The move to Newark (circa 1919) — 54
   Phil takes over — 56

VI Betrothals — 59
- A shidduch — 59
- A night out with the family (circa 1946) — 61
- Milton marries Anne (1937) — 62
- Bea marries Herman (1938) — 63
- Phil marries Jeanne (1944) — 64
- Til death do us part — 65

VII Sorrow — 69
- In memoriam (circa 1948) — 69
- Abe's death — 70
- Sophie marries Izzy (circa 1957) — 71

VIII Siblings — 75
- Celebrating together (circa 1962) — 75
- Where's Louis? (circa 1950) — 77
- Beach lovers (circa 1946) — 79
- Louis speaks back — 81

IX Grandchildren — 85
- Mother's Day Lunch (circa 1959) — 85
- Gefilted — 87
- Remembering Nana — 88
- Cousin COVID gathering — 91

X Thanksgiving — 93
- 101 North Frontenac (circa 1962) — 93
- Arnold and Alan perform — 95
- Pigeon poo — 98

XI Endings — 101
- A hard life — 101
- A failure of heart — 101
- Shrinking spaces — 103
- Ultimatum — 104
- Seashore Gardens — 106

XII Nana and Me	**109**
Leaning in to Sophie (circa 1956)	109
Nana's breasts	110
Cry baby	112
Becoming Nana	113
Cashmere sweater and pearls (circa 2023)	114
General References	**117**
Acknowledgements	**119**
About the Author	**122**

Author's Note

Preamble

This book is a tribute to the memory of my paternal grandmother, Sophie Kamler. It rises from a belief that Sophie was never accorded the witness and praise she deserved. She was never remembered as courageous for her journey out of the pogroms of Poland, at the tender age of 14, to early 20th century America. Like the lives of countless other remarkable women whose histories have been passed over, hers was a story never embellished, or lauded, or told from one generation to the next.

Sophie was born in 1893 in the small provincial town of Płońsk, Russia. As empires expanded and contracted, national borders dissolved and reformed. By the time Sophie left Płońsk in 1907, it was located in Poland. Like so many, Sophie was born into flux and turbulent times. Like so many desperate to flee pogroms and poverty, Sophie sought refuge in the United States. Whether state-sponsored or facilitated by a loosening of government control, continuing waves of antisemitic violence launched a massive human migration from Eastern Europe. By 1900, New York City—Sophie's destination— embraced more

Poles than any city except Warsaw, and more Jews than any other city in the world.

So, it is fair to ask: Was Sophie's departure different from others who fled oppression and sought a better life? Is her tale more heroic? Probably not, but her story is at least as courageous. Sophie's 'early' exit meant our family was not decimated by the Holocaust. I now live in Melbourne, a city with one of the highest concentrations of Holocaust survivors in the world. Many of my peers are children of survivors, while I am not.

I escaped that life-destroying trauma thanks to Sophie. Her children were first-generation-born Americans, because she was determined to escape an antisemitic hell. Did she see what was coming? Did she find the fortitude to leave her mother, when she herself was still a child, in order to escape all that she hated in small town Płońsk? She did. With fierce determination.

As a child I knew nothing of Sophie's story. I understood she had emigrated from Poland, but I had no grasp of her passage or the hardships endured. That is, until 1982, when my world upended—the year my mother died from ravaging cancer at age 58. I made it home to the United States just-in-time to see her before she died—a devastating six weeks alive between diagnosis and death. And I would return to Australia later—lost, untethered, broken by the theft of death. Immediately after the funeral our family sat *shiva* at my sister's home. Then I boarded a bus to Atlantic City to see Sophie.

We met at her daughter Bea's home in Margate, New Jersey, where she then lived. She was 89 and still mobile; strong mentally, but easily tired. I turned on the tape recorder and Sophie talked for over two hours, lapsing into Yiddish from time to time, until exhausted. Bea was in the room with us, prompting her mother for details she'd omitted, sometimes translating the Yiddish. 'Barbara doesn't understand Ma, speak English.'

What I discovered in that conversation shocked me—her resolve to survive, to bring her mother and seven siblings to America—to keep going, no matter what. When Sophie finished speaking, she asked, *This is what you want from me? It's enough? More* than enough. I needed her story to salve my loss, but received far more—a history, new knowledge, a connection to a past I dimly knew. In time I transcribed Sophie's account and emailed the transcript to my family, who shared my amazement. That was over 40 years ago. I have replayed the tape, reread the transcript, tried to craft poems from her words often, without success.

But now, as I reach my late 70s, I feel the press of Sophie's words, and the need to bring her forward in time, to craft a telling that lets the story transcend the woman who told it—and at the same time catch her more fully inside herself. I need to leave behind a trace of the tale that evokes such resonance for me.

Like Sophie, I am a traveller, I too left the country of my birth and have lived most of my life in a foreign place. In 1972, I journeyed to Australia for a two-year adventure, with no intention of staying or settling. Like her, I left home alone—beset neither by poverty nor antisemitism, but compelled nevertheless to go. I believed mine was an adventure, a temporary trip; Sophie knew hers was forever. Each visit I made back to New Jersey, she implored me to stay. As did my father, her youngest son, who never accepted my leaving America as anything but a betrayal. And still I stayed where I had run to.

For years I believed Sophie was upset because I reversed her journey. She struggled to get to America; I struggled to stay away. Yet now I see a palimpsest, the tracing of a line, the imprint of her life inside mine. I too journeyed; I too forged a new life, birthed a fine child, and in time found a good man to love, and be loved by. And now, in this last quarter of my life, I must write her down—with all the complexity and contradiction of any telling. I see Sophie, full-bosomed, corseted, forging ahead—surviving. As she did. As we did. Each in her own time and place.

> She stands before me
> and behind me travelling
> alone through unknown
> terrain and pain she holds up
> a mirror to show the way

Resources for writing

Sophie is a multi-voiced, mixed genre narrative. It is a collage comprised of 47 vignettes to tell the story of my grandmother from a variety of perspectives. My intent is to highlight the many truths that comprise a life. No story is ever singular; no person holds the only version. Although my interview with Sophie in 1982 is the pivot that spurred me to write this book, I wanted other stories to sit alongside hers, to get at the complexity and contradictions of her life.

Sophie's version is a powerful tale, and I am her advocate. I like inhabiting her words and writing from the taped recording—trying to capture her way of speaking, the spitfire—to let her come alive on the page. But she was not an easy woman. When she says over and over, *what a mother I was!* it is true, but not simply congratulatory.

She was brave—but also tough, often abrupt, a no-nonsense Nana. Sophie's children are no longer alive, and I'm not certain they would speak candidly if they were. So, I have relied on my own memories and those of my siblings and cousins, Sophie's other grandchildren. We are the last generation who knew her well—she is a shadowy presence for our children and grandchildren. For many she is completely unknown.

My cousins have offered new information, filling in gaps, prompting insights as I viewed Sophie across the family constellation, not just from the vantage point of my immediate family of five. Our media were WhatsApp calls, emails, recorded conversations. But on more than one occasion, after an uneasy confidence was shared, a 'please don't write about this' followed. Family secrets lie deep and do not like to be disturbed. I have honoured those confidences and fought against my own worn-out groove—replaying tensions with my father, Phil, Sophie's youngest child. The old feelings exist, they are detailed in *Leaving New Jersey*, that is enough. Still, they seep through this tale, but I hope with greater forgiveness and understanding.

Writing about family is always risky. An eminent poet once advised me, 'The only way to avoid the calumny of family disapproval is to write of the dead, not the living.' And yet this advice is not straightforward; even when the protagonists are no longer alive, their descendants will have different viewpoints; they may be disturbed by the version offered here. Stories of sibling and parental discord are rife in the chronicles of writers' lives. I have attended many book launches where the writer sheepishly murmurs, 'Sorry Mum and Dad, you won't like this.'

My approach is to juxtapose stories *about* Sophie with those of *her own* telling—to structure the book so they might speak to one another. While I allow Sophie to speak directly to the reader in first person, her monologue is inevitably shaped by me. The transcript of any interview is full of repetition, false starts, discontinuous thought and confusion. I have crafted Sophie's account by using *her* words, but paring them back with an ear to retaining her syntax, her Polish-accented English, the lapse into Yiddish, the *oy yoy yoy* of complaint sitting below the surface. All her words included here I have italicized as the main quotations in this book. Other quotes appear in non-italics inside quotation marks.

I have, of course, shaped the stories *about* Sophie as well. At times I use direct quotes from my cousins and siblings, and at others meld their memories with mine, as narrator, into a series of vignettes evoking particular times, places or events. Read together, they create a discontinuous narrative, not always chronological, but full of gaps, emotion, reflections and, I hope, love.

More than words

I have divided *Sophie* into 12 parts, organised around her life cycle. As matriarch of our tribe, it seemed fitting to foreground her perspective: her departure from Poland and arrival in America; her marriage to Abe; growing a family and a family business together; her relations with siblings, with her children and grandchildren; and as she aged, the gradual loss of loved ones, health, space and horizon. Each part features, as far as possible, vignettes of Sophie speaking, presented in italics, alongside the narrated stories by which we remember her.

But the visual modality also plays a pivotal role in my storytelling. I place one family photo at the beginning of each chapter, or close to, and from time to time an additional image at the end. I have avoided the practice of lumping pictures together in the centre of the book, although I am aware how the influence of publishing economies often prevails in this practice. Here the photos mark different phases of Sophie's life. They are an invitation to the reader to engage with my grandmother and her descendants even more directly, to create also a visual history.

My use of photographs has been influenced by Janet Malcolm's *Still Pictures,* a visually-based memoir which assembles a powerful portrait of her New York childhood; and Roland Barthes' *Camera Lucida*, in particular his concept of the *studium* and the *punctum*. I understand the *studium* to be that which is represented and placed before the camera lens, the person and objects we know as real. But sometimes the *punctum* also arises, the detail that punctures composure, like an unexpected flash that takes us outside the frame of the photograph. It may be a gesture, a facial expression, an item of clothing, an angle of repose that, 'rises from the scene, shoots out of it like an arrow and pierces me.' (p 26). And so I also comment on details that disturb and encourage me to speculate about the past. These wonderings also become part of the story here told.

A partial family tree

It is always confusing to keep the details of other people's family clear. In Russian novels the naming practices can confuse, but even in the most simple of family structures, the who's who, and how they are related, can interfere with the flow of narrative. I include here a partial family tree of four generations—giving prominence to Sophie, her children and grandchildren—those who appear most centrally in this telling. The absences are many and have nothing to do with the importance of family members. Stories of Sophie's great-grandchildren and great-great grandchildren will have to wait for another time.

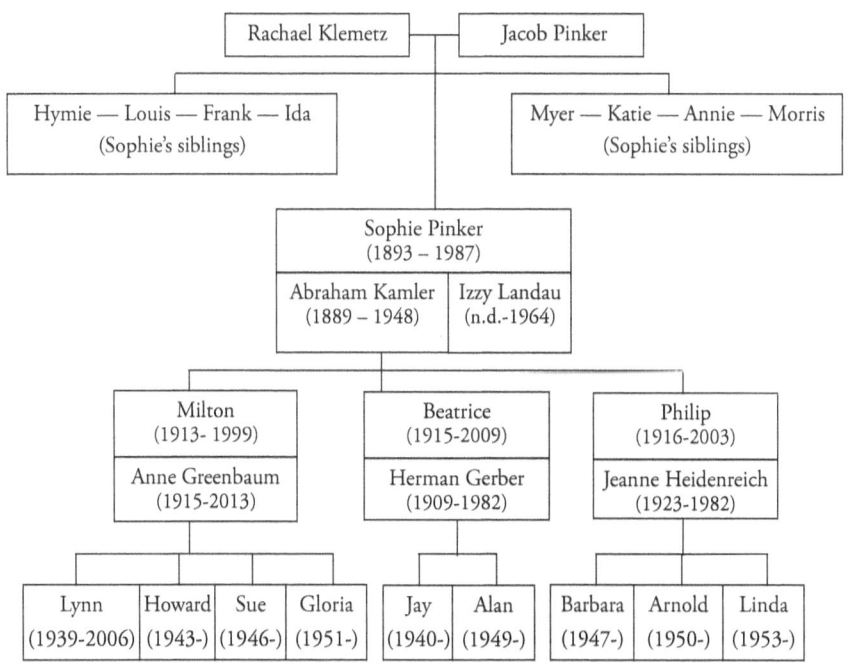

I Departure

Fleeing Płońsk (1907)

I was born in Płońsk. But when I was five my parents moved to London and I started public school there. Canon Street School until fifth grade, that's all my education. But Mama didn't want to stay, it wasn't Jewish enough for her, so she took us back to Płońsk. She insisted. My father refused. We were seven kids and Mama pregnant with twins. That's when my father left us destitute in Płońsk, he didn't write, didn't send money. Nothing. And he went to America. I tell you it's a sin what he did to us.

I don't want to think about the way we were. Starving, no money, no place to live. Mama stuck in a shack at the back of her brother's place with the little ones. My sister Annie she sent to her mother, me and Myer she farmed out to Bubbe, my father's mother. She couldn't care for us all. How could I forgive a man who left his family, left me prey to those boys who hunted and hounded me screaming, 'Dirty Jew, get out of here!'

So, I coaxed my Bubbe, she should write to him to take me out of this hellhole or I'm gonna' run. Where I'm gonna' run I don't know, but I couldn't take the antisemitism. I couldn't take it. For months and days, I hollered she should give me the address for my father, I begged her, crying. She was the only person who knew where he was.

Then one day—a miracle. Two tickets arrived for me and my younger brother, Myer. No money, no letter, just passage for two to America in steerage class—where the poor people go, down in the cargo hold.

He was just 13, me 14. The night we left Mama broken-hearted I'll never forget. How could I go without her? How could she and the children survive? Mama's uncle found a carriage to take us to Hamburg to board the boat. But right away they separated us, me with the women, Myer with the men. He was such a shy boy, not too smart. I couldn't rest 'til I found him.

I was searching for him, up and down the deck, but it was slippery, the passageways dark. I fell. Plonked down 32 steps. Tseklapt! Oy! They took me to the ship's hospital—bandaged black and blue but already it was good. They gave me food—no more herring and potatoes. And I spoke a little English, you know, they liked me.

But Myer still didn't know where I was. I was talking to the sailors and nurses to find him. I knew he was scared. Finally, when they understood what I wanted, they located Myer and brought him to me. I was the happiest person living to see him. For two weeks we were on that boat and I was terrible sick, hanging on to the address where my father lived.

We arrived Ellis Island on Thanksgiving Day, 1907. But they wouldn't let us off the boat until the next day—my face was so bruised you know, my eyes all black, so they examined me tip to toe and I passed, Got zay dank. I saw my father below waiting for us with a cousin, Sam Kane. But he looked so tight and sour, no smile on his face for his two eldest kids, dressed in rags, come all the way from that hellhole Płońsk.

Płońsk dismantled

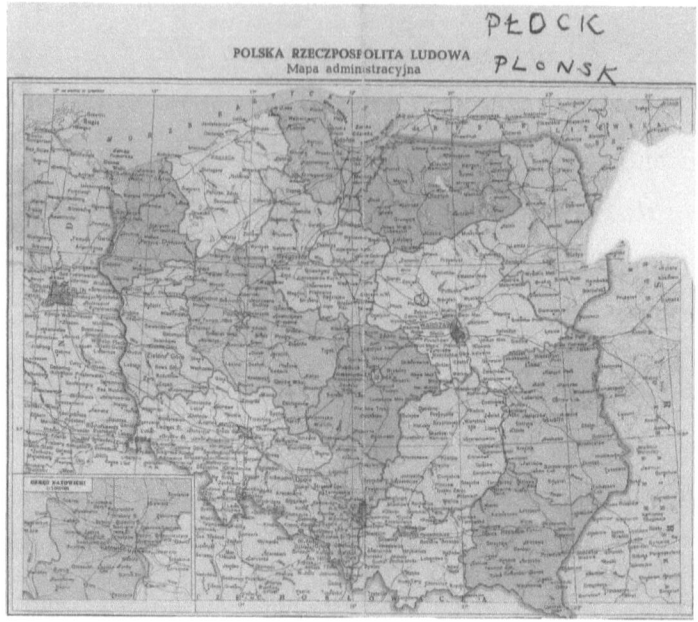

Płońsk is our point of origin in Central Poland, 60 kilometres west of Warsaw—the town where Sophie and Abe were born and grew up with their families. But how surprising to find this administrative map of Poland buried amongst my father's papers. It is a slightly tattered, yellowing coloured plate, with Płońsk circled lightly in pen and in the right corner the words PLONSK and PŁOCK, scribed in my father's handwriting. The map shows 17 provinces or voivodeships (there are now 16) and the legend details boundaries, railways, roads, canals and swamps notated in English and four other languages: French (Pologne), German (Polen), Russian (Плоньск) and Spanish (Polonoa). The torn corner suggests it was ripped out of an atlas or Polish compendium, torn perhaps by my father when he ventured to Warsaw in 1973.

When Sophie left Płońsk in 1907, Jews still had a strong presence, the population evenly divided—Poles residing in the more rural and remote areas, and Jews around the city centre and market square. Although Sophie spoke of her exile as an individual plagued by antisemitism, her experience was not unique. Multiple waves of pogroms swept across Eastern Europe from the 1880s. Intense anti-Jewish alliances and violence—the looting of Jewish property, murder and rape—made life intolerable.

More than two million Jews entered the United States between 1881 and 1924, most clustered in urban districts, like the Lower East side of New York, where Sophie settled. A large number from Płońsk also emigrated to Palestine, seeking a homeland and safety from oppression, in what is called the Second Aliyah (1904–1913). Amongst the most famous was David Ben-Gurion, who left Płońsk a year after Sophie and in 1948 became the first Prime Minister of Israel.

Today Płońsk survives with 20,000+ inhabitants. However, the decimation of the Jewish community who remained in Płońsk prior to World War II was merciless and swift. In 1939 the Germans invaded, a year later they imprisoned Jews into a ghetto, and by 1942 they liquidated the remaining populace, sending 12,000 to Auschwitz. Had Sophie remained she would have been 45 years old and mother of three, assuming Abe also stayed and they married. It may be dramatic speculation to wonder if the family could have survived, but it seems unlikely. I am reminded often that Sophie's crossing in 1907 was our saving, our lives ensured.

Płońsk revisited (1973)

It was 1973 when my father Phil, Sophie's youngest son, flew to Warsaw. He had finished his business in Hungary, meeting with the key manufacturer of his bicycles, and had a few days to spare. At his accommodation in the Europejski Hotel, he inquired whether he might find an interpreter and driver to take him to Płońsk, the birthplace of his parents. The young concierge was more than accommodating. As he was free the next day, he volunteered his services and organised transportation with his friend, a taxi driver.

At 9am Saturday morning they set off on a westerly course toward the German border, 60 kilometres from Warsaw. My father's quest began at city hall. The concierge told the officer-in-charge: 'I have an American here whose mother and father were born in this town. He's looking for any records of his family. Can you help us?' At first the man prevaricated. As Poland had been controlled over the decades by Russians, Germans, by Hungary and Austria, the records were in four different languages stored away in a warehouse. And hard to locate. My father did not believe him. 'Well,' he asked through the concierge, 'is anyone of the Jewish faith still in Płońsk that I might talk to?'

The official sent them to an address a block and a half south of town. A four-story middle-European dwelling centred around a courtyard. They entered through a large archway and ascended the stairway on the interior of the house to the fourth floor. A woman in her 50s greeted them, apprehensively. 'Is there anyone here who might remember this American man's family?' 'You need to speak to my husband', she said, and she sent her 12-year-old son to accompany them to a flour mill nearby. Her husband was the miller, covered head to foot in white flour dust. When he asked what they wanted, the interpreter told the story again. 'Was there anyone in the town who might remember?'

'What was the name of the family?', the miller asked. KAMLER. With this the miller turned to study my father's face. He stared intently, as if cataloguing a lifetime of images, and then nodded. 'I know the name Kamler, yes. There was a large family here. This man's grandfather was extremely active in the synagogue—a learned man, very orthodox, he had nine children. Most went to America, some to Israel. I remember he owned a small shop that manufactured caps.'

At this point it was my father who turned white. This was precisely what his father Abe had told him. Abe's brother Anshul, who lived in Linden, New Jersey, remained a cap maker after he migrated to America. Every morning he'd take the 7am train to the lower East Side of New York to work in a small cap factory—until he died.

My father and the miller then attempted to converse directly, using a mix of Yiddish and German. When the Nazis came to Płońsk at the beginning of the war, the Jewish population was cordoned off into a ghetto, sent to labour camps and later to Auschwitz. Only four Jewish families remained. 'I was one of those four', the miller said; 'I was hidden by farmers for the duration of the war. But those four families all intermarried with Poles, so all Jewish life ended in Płońsk.'

My father asked him to write the family name in Polish. 'Not too far from what you told me', he said.

K A M L A R Z. 'We drove around for a while,' my father recalled, 'and I bought postcards to send to my mother and her siblings, Annie and Hymie and Louis, so they would receive mail from Płońsk. I don't think I've ever had an experience like it, or will ever again.'

As I reflect on my father's experience in Płońsk, I find it remarkable that the son who felt ever unfavoured by his mother was the one who took the journey back to their roots, to honour the place of origin where the family began.

II Arrival

Sophie finds work

I couldn't bear being with my father. Straight away he put me to work in his tailor shop to pull bastings from the men's coats. It's illegal; you think he cares? Every day the Inspector came, he hid me in the toilet so he won't get in trouble. You can imagine how I hated him, such a temper, so mean.

I begged my cousin Sam Kane to take me in. I'll never forget him as long as I live. He and his wife owned a hat store on Clinton Street. At first his wife was nice, she wanted to teach me. That's good. But soon enough I could see what she wanted was a servant—to clean and cook and shop for her, to do everything. But I'm not that kind, you know. I begged Sam, 'Please find me some work. I need something.' By that time, I was maybe 15. He had a friend on Barnett Street, Mr Cohen, with a shop that made feather boas. 'Maybe he could teach you,' he says. So Sam struck a deal with the man. 'Four weeks my cousin will work for nothing', Sam says, 'I guarantee you that. You don't pay her nothing. But she's smart. Treat her right, teach her the trade.'

Four weeks I worked very hard. I walked from Bond Street in the Bowery all the way to the river each day and I learned. When four weeks were up, I said, 'Mr Cohen, from today I'll do piece work like the other girls—for a wage.' He screamed, 'You greenhorn. You're telling me you want pay? You can work, but I won't give you a cent. You don't know the trade yet.'

I knew the trade. Believe me I knew better than the girls he paid. But I didn't say nothing to him and I didn't want to complain to Sam. Next day I was at Leibl's house, my father's brother. You know I often went back and forth between Sam and Leibl. They knew it was bad with my father and they took me in. Sometimes I stayed by Amy Wagner, my friend from school in London. Her mother was kind to me, she also took me in. If my father came, she'd throw him out. 'Get out of here, you can't have that child in your house! Go!'

At Leibl's I saw an ad in the paper: 'London Feather Company, Kent Street and Broadway. Experienced ostrich feather sewers wanted'. Ich bin nisht geven a sewer. I was never a sewer. What did I know? I only learned to sew six inches for the boas at Cohen's—but the ostrich feather for the hat needs 36 inches. I thought to myself, I'll go anyway. A nice young man at the company asked me, 'So where did you work before?' I thought if I gave Cohen's name, it would be trouble for me. But I remembered swinging in the park on Cambridge Road in London when I was a girl. I went to public school there til the fifth grade, that's where I learned to speak English.

So I told him, 'Cambridge Road.' He frowned and smiled. 'There's no factory there for ostrich feathers.' 'It's a little place, quite unknown,' I said. 'But we made good stuff.'

He looked me up and down and smiled—hot nich ongekikt. He sees how I'm dressed—a schlepper, rags for clothes, no coat. I had nothing! My English not so good, but I remember his words: 'I like your nerve to tell me in Cambridge Road there's a factory. I like your nerve. Here's a feather to make up. If you do it right, I'll give you a place.'

A nice Irish lady took me to a private office. She took apart all the pieces and said 'Now begin!' I started to scrape the feather and she smiled. She knew I didn't know how. 'You look like a smart girl,' she said. 'I'll make that feather up for you and you say you did it. Come back tomorrow, mind your business, don't speak to nobody and ask for me. I'm sure you'll learn quickly.'

And that's the feather she showed to the man. Such luck I had that day! Next morning I returned and she taught me—do this, do that, put it together, that's how. And I did it right. She said, 'It's wonderful!'

That first week I made eight dollars. Can you imagine? By me it was $8,000. When my father heard I'm earning money, he wanted to take me home right away. *Gonif.* But Sam threw him out. 'Get out of this house before I hit you', he said. 'You leave Sophie alone.' He protected me.

Friends for life (circa 1908)

Sophie loved this photo and proudly displayed it on her sideboard, *This is me and my friend*. Although there is no writing on the back, it is fair to speculate this friend (on the left) is Annie Wagner, the girl she first met at primary school in London and amazingly later found again in New York, a friendship she treasured.

It is striking how the bodies of these young girls are aligned—Annie's arm around Sophie's shoulder, Sophie's left arm reaching across to hold Annie's hand. Such a moment speaks of closeness, an entwined holding. Their dainty feet are garbed in identical white t-straps, flowers strewn at their feet. Obviously shot in a photographic studio, it is unlikely Sophie had money for such an extravagance. Perhaps Annie's mother paid, wanting to gift something to this young girl, working so hard to survive and make her way on her own. We know she opened her home to Sophie for respite and safe haven—a bed, a roof, time out from her father.

Yet it is almost impossible for us, Sophie's grandchildren, to recognise her—waist cinched so tightly, white full-length bouffant gown with high ruffled collar and long white gloves. It is the only image we have after she arrived in America, before marrying Abe, yet it is the tiny waist that most disturbs. We only knew Nana as full-bodied, sturdy, with a solid waist and ample breasts. Her bunioned feet always shod in thick-heeled, sensible black shoes.

As I peer at this image, I have an irreverent thought. Might this be a photographic trick, the faces of the girls transposed onto the body of others, as in amusement park photos? Perhaps the fancy attire was provided by the photographer? For all the deception photos allow, we might imagine Sophie as a sheltered girl of comfortable means, enjoying a day out with a friend. Two southern belles in plantation finery? Young debutantes before the ball? But here is the lie: There is no party, no ball, Sophie is not carefree, or of any means at all until she labours to make a living and bring her mother and siblings to America.

Abe finds Sophie

I was in America for just two weeks when Leibl came looking for me. 'Sophie host shoin a chusen fun Płońsk?' I said, 'Sure, I knew a boy in Płońsk—by the name Abe.' I was a good-looking girl, the boys ran after me. 'Well,' my uncle says, 'that boy is looking for you. He's asking around.'

At first, I couldn't understand what he's talking. I remember when I told Abe I'm going to America he said, 'I'm gonna' come too. I'll steal my brother's ticket and go by his name, Anshul. We Płońskers always find each other.' Nu, what does he know? He had no money, his mother had died, how could he come to America? When his father remarried the wife chased out all the three boys, they had nothing. Nothing.

But as I walked out from my uncle's house—there he was, Abe standing by the steps. In New York! How did he find me? Well, he said he would. After he arrived, he went to his sister's house, his sister knew my

Uncle Leibl and my uncle found me. That's how. I was very happy to see him. Thank God he got out of that dump in Płońsk!

Every morning Abe followed me around and walked me to my work at the Feather Company. But when my father saw me going with him, he nearly killed him. 'You go with a greenhorn just off the boat,' he screamed. 'He has nothing! Nothing!' It was true. Abe was so poor if he wanted a cigarette, I used to give him a quarter, he should buy a couple of cigarettes.

He found work in a bike shop on Dillard Street. The owner was a Gallicianobus, a religious man from Galicia, so he didn't open the shop Saturday, it was Shabbas. But after sundown, he demanded Abe work until midnight—for five dollars a week! Such a mean boss to my Abe, terrible. Abe suffered but he never complained.

You know I stayed at that Feather Company for two years. I made such good money I sent for Mama with all the children—they should all come to America: Annie, Frank, Morris, Katie, Ida, and the twins Hymie and Louis. I brought them all. My mother and father started living together again and he took a place in Pitt Street—near the Williamsburg Bridge, with *all the kids. She had no money. Where could she go? But it was hell. You have your mother and your father; you think maybe something will go right already. I hoped. But no. He was mad at Mama for returning to Płońsk. She was mad at him for leaving us poor. It was hell all the time.*

III Marriage

Partners for life (circa 1911)

It is the coming together of Sophie Pinker and Abraham Kamler that marks our beginning. A quiet determination emanates from the photograph as they sit close, heads gently touching. How serious they look, how innocent, softly held in sepia tone. They seem to look ahead to a future they cannot yet imagine, to a family they will create. Sophie is perfectly coiffed, Abe handsome in suit and tie. But my eye turns to the locket at Sophie's neck. Whose photo rests within? Is it Abe who will stand by her for the next 37 years, be true to her until he dies so prematurely? Or her mother Rachael, devoted to keeping her children alive in the most desperate circumstances of poverty?

Here Abe and Sophie lean in to one another. He is there for her. He will do whatever she needs in this new world of America. He is hers and she is his, as long as he does as she says. He will work and she will direct. She will rule and he will say yes.

Sophie left Płońsk to find a new life, desperate to escape the gnawing antisemitism. Abe left Poland to find her. And to Sophie's amazement, he did. In the squalid brownstones of the lower east side of New York, in the Jewish scuttlebutt of who knew who, and who lived where, Abe found Sophie on the steps of her uncle's house. Just two weeks after she arrived. A small miracle or perhaps it was *beshert*, destined to be.

Wedding day

Abe and I married on November 20, 1911. I was 18. I remember like it would be now. Paris Lyceum 206 East Broadway New York. My mother invited all the landsman from Płońsk. Five hundred people. I didn't know who, they didn't know me. But when the neighbourhood discovered a wedding—people paid the hatcheck a quarter to go in and eat. The man at the hall made such a success that night he gave me a gallon of wine. I don't drink.

But a week before the wedding my father told me, 'es oys kleiden die kinder. If you buy clothes for the children we'll come to the wedding. They should look decent. Otherwise, I won't come—none of us will.' Such a nerve. So, I bought shoes and clothes for the kids. Who else? I paid for the wedding. Who then? Would he pay? Alright. We'll leave that.

We brought Abe's old grandfather to the wedding. He was living in a home in East Broadway. End of the night Mama says, 'You take the old man home to sleep in your house'. What could I do? We lived in an apartment for six dollars a month, Mama lived downstairs, but she had no room. Abe and I slept on the floor, the grandfather slept in our bed. This was my honeymoon. By morning I saw the old man davening and I wanted to give him a good breakfast afterwards. But not a crumb in the house—every cent we spent on the wedding. So, I got the idea to see Abe's partner in the business where they hired bicycles. 'I'll borrow a dollar from Jaekel,' I thought.

And what did Jaekel say to me? 'One day you're married and you're here for the money already? I don't want no woman coming to bother me.' Well, I got so mad. 'Listen Jaekel! Why are you so excited? You're afraid I won't give it back? I want a dollar, don't say another word.' I bought bagels, lox and cream cheese on Hester Street and gave the old man a full breakfast. One dollar was like $50 back then.

But that dollar hurt me. I didn't tell anything to Abe right away. But a few days later I told him, 'You throw Jaekel out. I'll be your partner. He's no good, such a lazy man, you do all the work'. Little by little I'm hammering. 'I don't want him—get him out—he's no good.'

Abe was mad at him because he opened up a mouth to me. But Abe wasn't the fighting kind. He told me to do it, he couldn't. I found Jake at the store: 'Now listen,

I can't say I don't like you, Jake. You're a nice man, but since you gave me those words about the dollar, I'll always look at you in a mean way. So, let's part. You pay me out.' 'No', he said, 'you pay me out.' In the end we split the stock. Jake bought a pushcart and moved to the Bronx. Abe and I remained in Division Street and we made a nice living. And now I was the partner.

No children

I was married eight weeks when I had such a pain—a tumour on the kidney. It happened so sudden; you know the kidney had to be removed. I was raised alone without a mother and always suffered my monthly period. But who should I tell? My father? Or Sam? I had nobody. At the clinic I saw a famous professor. The operation cost thousands, but he donated his time for poor patients. Eight weeks after my wedding the kidney was removed. And the doctor said, 'No children. You'll die if you have a child.'

Well, I was pregnant right away with Milton so the doctor threw me out. He said, 'I saved your life once, I can't do anything for you now.' You know, you can only die once. I died on that boat alone without my mother—and still I'm living. I had Milton, then Bea, then 16 months later Phil. I'll never forget how terrible—a whole week in labour with Milton. I still had a tube draining from the kidney and I begged them for an abortion, but they wouldn't. They said, 'You shouldn't have done it, but it's done. Abortion is impossible, you'll have to lay'. I lay nine months until I came to the labour. *Az men daft lebyn.*

If it's fated for you to live, you'll live. When a person is born there's a date and you got to wait until that date when you're going to die. They watched me closely. I wanted to throw myself out the window. They gave no drugs at that time. But that doctor, if he's dead, he should turn over 100 times in his grave. Why he let me live, he should have killed me. He and his wife—a nurse—they wouldn't leave me. They knew I might do something to myself. But I had to live and suffer.

IV Motherhood

Sophie and her kids (circa 1920)

Sophie stands proud and straight, the pillar supporting her three offspring. Her hands rest on the shoulders of her two eldest. To the right Milton, the favoured son, expected to bring *naches* to the family as a dentist, a professional man. To the left Bea, the daughter whose desires and interests will, in time, become almost indistinguishable from those of her mother. Both lean into Sophie, smiling, heads tilted as if to please.

The photo itself is creased and crumpled, much like the garden, overgrown and unkempt. Clumps of grass rise to an old splintering fence; a creeping vine grows wild. The setting is most likely the back of the bicycle shop on South Orange Avenue, where the family will settle after the move to New Jersey. It is unlikely there was time or money to look after a garden.

If pictures foretell, this photograph catches Bea where she will stay, at her mother's side—united as one. But it also catches my father Phil, Sophie's youngest, where he will stay. Separate. His small hands grasp the steering wheel with determination, as if he might drive away at any moment. Yet his facial expression most resembles hers—squinting into the sun, lips parted in an almost smile. Sophie described him as: *a good boy, easiest to birth, not too demanding.* But perhaps he refused to pose for the photo unless he sat in his car. That seems conceivable to those of us who knew him as a father—getting his way.

Yet it is the lack of physical contact between my father and his mother that I find unsettling, a precursor of relations between them. As an adult Phil was a dutiful son, but distant. Our family visited Sophie regularly, most often on Sundays. We remember Phil on the phone, jiggling coins in his pocket shouting 'Ma, don't tell me what to do' or hanging up abruptly. We never knew what the problem was, it just *was*. Now I wonder how deeply we were affected, steeped in his frustration, sensing discord but not understanding why. And never hearing admiration for our Nana.

The best mother

When we got away from New York and moved to New Jersey, Milton was six, Bea four, and Philly three. We had a nice apartment at the back of the shop in Newark. Not luxury but nice—a living room, dining room and two bedrooms upstairs. The boys slept in twin beds and Bea in the dining room. I made sure they were all comfortable and had everything they needed, a good education.

They went to public school—the three together, and came home at lunchtime. I prepared a hot meal, but you know if I was busy in front with the store, sometimes they didn't eat their proper lunch. If I saw that bottle of milk still left on the table, I walked to the school with the bottle. When the principal saw me, he yelled, 'Get the Kamler kids, she's here!' I watched until they drank—all three—in the middle of my business day. What a mother I was! Did I deserve what I got?

The eldest son

Milton attended New York University his first year. But his friend Morris Deitch went to the University of Michigan. And that friend talked Milton into going to Michigan. It was terrible. I couldn't afford to pay tuition and board there. Papa was sick already from the heart attack and things were bad. But Milton said, 'I don't care if you can't help me Ma, I'll go to work. I'd rather work than go back to NYU.' Ven ich hob gehert. When I heard that it killed me.

My only aim in life—my children should have what I didn't have, best of everything. A good education. So, I said to myself, 'I don't care how hard I have to work, he'll go to Michigan.' When he left home I couldn't eat or sleep. How could a boy who never travelled further than from Newark to New York go so far away? To me Michigan was the end of the world. Ek velt. Where was it? How did I know? I got sick, a nervous breakdown. The doctor said, 'The only thing to cure you—either the crazy house or travel to see how your darling boy is living.'

I took Bea on the Greyhound bus to Michigan. I had the address where he was living, but when I saw that place—*siz geven shrecklech*—a terrible place, dark and small, not clean. I asked if there were any Jewish people in the town? They sent me to a grocery store five blocks away and the man there asked right away, 'Are you here because your boy flunked?' He was starting to pity me already. 'No, nothing like that,' I said. 'Can you tell me if any Jewish people here can take in my son and his friend for board?'

He told me of a widow in Green Street who did laundry for the professors. 'Maybe she can help, if she has a permit.' I found this Mrs Silver. She came out from the laundry basement and gave me the same pity. 'Oy I'm so sorry your boy flunked.' Everybody right away thought that. She made hot tea. 'Now tell me what is it you want.'

'I have two boys here and I want a place where they should eat and sleep with good meals, just like mother's care. I'll pay you as much as you want.'

'Oh', she says, 'you're just God from heaven sent. I'm barely making a living from that poor little laundry.

If I can get a permit, I'll take your two boys.' I was so happy to hear her words. I left a note for Milton he should call this number after his classes. He was shocked to know I came. 'What happened Ma? What brings you here? Is something wrong with Dad?' I said, 'Nothing's wrong with Dad. Just come for supper and bring Morris too.'

We had a beautiful supper Mrs Silver prepared. I stayed overnight with Bea to make a price with the woman. You know she didn't have any money and me—now I'm the millionaire! That cured me. When I saw Milton had a beautiful room with a little alcove to study and good meals I felt better right away. I couldn't stay because I left a sick husband home. But Milton was satisfied. That's the kind of mother I was.

The only daughter

Bea grew up with her siblings in northern New Jersey, proximate to New York City. The city was always within reach—just an hour away by train, 50 minutes by car. From the youngest age, Bea was held in its thrall. She loved Manhattan and all it offered—music, theatre, opera, galleries, excitement.

So, marriage in her 20s shocked her foundations, catapulting her to Tuckerton, a quiet community in

South Jersey where her husband Herman's family was well established. The Gerbers were bigshots in town, the Gerber Department Store an institution since 1921. But Bea hated the place from the start—too parochial, too small, too far from her mother and the urban world she loved.

Most weekends she travelled back and forth to Sophie and Abe's, without Herman—young son Jay in tow. They left Friday afternoons after school. Three-and-a-half hours on the Greyhound bus, through an array of small towns (no freeway back then) until they reached the end of the line, Newark. Abe picked them up at the bus station and ferried daughter and grandson to modest living at their 21st street apartment in Irvington: living room, dining room, kitchen, one bathroom, one bedroom and pull-out beds for the visitors. This routine continued for years until Bea became pregnant with her second son, Alan. Then she moved in with Sophie for the entire duration of her pregnancy.

Looking back, Jay is convinced his mother had Alan as a way of going back to live with her mother. No one seemed to worry about removing Jay from his friends and well-loved community for the year. He attended grade four at Berkeley Terrace Elementary School in Irvington and a bedroom was created for him in Sophie's living room.

He was an adaptable kid, he made friends and fitted in. Herman visited on occasional weekends. But after giving birth, Bea made up her mind. The family would start again in Atlantic City, a larger, more cosmopolitan community, just 30 commuter miles from Herman's law practice. Herman agreed and found a massive four-story house on Delancey Place—a 'white elephant,' the agents called it—and he bought it for a bargain. Bea never liked it—the house was too vast to look after, too many steps to climb—not good, she believed, for her heart.

Tough love

I've been wondering about the casualties of Sophie's desire to make good in a new country—to ensure her children achieved more than she and Abe? It is the immigrant's dream, well documented and theorised across cultures and centuries by so many writers.

Sophie was adamant her children would have the best education and be college-educated. She worked hard to ensure they had music lessons. Phil played tenor saxophone, Milton violin, and Bea piano. But music was a pastime, not a career. When Phil was in his senior year of high school and invited to travel with his orchestra over summer, Sophie forbade him.

I used to cry and beg him to stop. I didn't approve. When he planned to go on the road I said, 'You're not gonna' go on no road. You want to make an orchestra, make an orchestra yourself here and play if you want to play.' He didn't go but he was mad.

In later years my father confided he would have liked to play saxophone professionally, but the remuneration was too poor. At his 80th birthday celebration, he invited old musician friends to play for the night, Tommy Dorsey swing band-style. Everyone danced and Phil was in his glory, also wistful. Milton also confided to daughter Gloria that he yearned to be a violinist—he loved playing music, listening to music and dancing. But he fulfilled his mother's dream of having a doctor in the family, a doctor of dentistry. Would Milton and Phil have been happier, less prone to frustration if they followed their hearts? We can only speculate.

Their sister Bea, educated at Newark Teachers' College, never worked outside the home after she married a professional man, except to do occasional substitute teaching. She was an avid fan of a radio soap opera about a sophisticated city girl who moved to a small town in the sticks and longed to be elsewhere—just as she longed for life in New York City. Longing and success intertwined, but at odds. Sophie expected her children to succeed, and they did, perhaps at the expense of other dreams.

V Business

The gangsters came

We had a good business in New York, on Division Street, between the Bowery and Canal Street. We made a nice living with the bicycles until the gangsters found Abe. They targeted the small shopkeepers, and if you refused to give money, they threatened. You had to give. But I didn't know until that Sunday morning. I already had my three kids and the carriage was outside by the window. I saw two men come into the shop, they picked the best bike and walked out. Abe was hiding in the corner. I yelled 'Abe, what's happening? Have you got a deposit?' And I started to scream. They heard me and came back into the shop— took out a knife.

We had a line of maybe 100 bicycles and they slashed ALL the tires. All the tires. I was hollering murder so they ran out, but Abe was so angry at me. 'I told you not to bother, not to mix in. Why did you?' And I said, 'What is it? I don't know what it is. Tell me what.' That was the first he confided—about the threats, the money he gave. I was shocked. 'You're standing here in such a dangerous place and you never say a word to me?'

When the police came, they wanted us to press charges against those two that slashed the tires. We walked to the police station, but those gangsters came up behind. 'If you open up a mouth and talk, we'll kill your three children.' We went home right away and didn't talk. I was scared. That's when I said, 'I'm not going to stay in this place no more Abe. If you want to stay, you stay. I'm gonna' take my three kids and move. Somewheres.' I didn't know where, but he saw I meant it.

The move to Newark (circa 1919)

Abe found a place for sale in Newark—49 South Orange Avenue, Newark. We had $5,000. At that time it was like a million. Abe had a friend from Poland and he had $5,000. So together we bought that place in Newark with the partner. I gave the business in New York to my brother-in-law Harry, my sister Annie's husband. Harry wasn't a mean guy, but gruff like them. He had a gun. If the gangsters came, he showed his gun. 'If you're not going to get out of here quick', he yelled, 'we'll carry you out.'

I was always afraid those gangsters shouldn't come to Newark and find us. They used to knock in the middle of the night. 'Abe, we need money'. How much did he give? $5. $10. I don't know. Enough to keep them away. Terrible.

But in Newark we made out very nice. Abe's friend was a nice fellow—they used to work in Europe together, they were good mechanics with the bicycles. But when I saw how he stood by the register while my husband slaved away on repairs all day long, I couldn't take it. Always trouble with the partner and Abe wouldn't say nothing. He was too easy and I couldn't fight with him.

So, I told my lawyer Greenfield, 'I can't do nothing with that partner of my husband, please talk to him.' Greenfield approached him and said, 'What's the use of arguing, you can't agree and the wife isn't satisfied. Make up in a good way and dissolve the partnership.

If you want to stay here, you pay Abe out. Or Abe can pay you out.' The partner agreed to go. 'I don't want no trouble', he said. 'I was always friends with both of them. I'll go somewhere else.' That's how it was. He went to Montclair; we remained in South Orange Avenue.

I worked hard with my husband. He was a good labourer, not a businessman. He liked to work, that's all. He knew more about bicycles than anybody in the whole city Newark. Everyone came to our store because Abe was such a good mechanic. And they came for the best price. If Abe saw a dollar profit, he accepted it. Good enough. I didn't see things that way. If I could make $10 profit I did. So, when a customer came in, I chased Abe to the back of the shop to let me do the talking.

Finally, after everything was good, the business was good, he had his first heart attack. One operation, then another, another. Then the tzurus really began.

Phil takes over

When Abe became too ill to work, it was my dad Phil who stepped up to run the family business. He left full-time studies at New York University and re-enrolled part-time at night—as many do now, but it was not common then. Later he left a promising position as an accountant with Price Waterhouse in New York.

Yet he never felt acknowledged for his effort or sacrifice. Never felt recognised for the canny way he took the small retail Kamler Cyclery in Newark and built it into Philkam Cycle, a wholesale distributor of bikes. Or how, in the '60s, he created a new entity, Kent International, where he designed, manufactured and imported his own brand of bicycle. Initially Kent bicycles were imported from Eastern Europe, then Japan and later China. Never, it seems, did Sophie acknowledge his success in becoming a major player in the American bicycle industry. And it irked him.

Yet he seemed driven by the same ambition that propelled his mother. He became the most financially astute of her three children, the most successful in material terms and well-recognised in the business world for his skill. Yet it chafed. What was it he needed from Sophie that she never gave? Perhaps his lifelong yearning was that of a small child, trying to wedge a place in his mother's arms? Aching for recognition.

After Abe died, Phil looked after Sophie's finances and put her on his payroll so she would receive social security benefits. He subsidised her income. But she was never satisfied with his contribution.

Some of us carry our abandonment so deeply

we are unable to see where we are. Or who we have become. Or forgive those we believe have abandoned us. I see my father's grief drifting across days and decades, soundlessly as snow, whispering: *you're not good enough…you are never enough.*

VI Betrothals

A shidduch

You know I made a shidduch for Milton with Anne. When I went to Michigan to make sure Milton had a good place to live, good home cooking, right away Mrs Silver told all her friends in Ann Arbor. 'This mother came all the way from Newark to look for a place for her boy. What a mother!! What a beautiful family it must be!' Her friend Mrs Greenbaum wanted to see what it was about and brought her two daughters to the house, Anne and Emma. Right away Milton fell in love with Anne. That was it. He was in love from the first he saw her. He was too young, but that's how they became man and wife.

And your parents, also from a shidduch by Anne. When your mother's sister Miriam married, she moved to Stuyvesant Avenue to the Irvington Garden Apartments. This was the same place where Milton and Anne already lived. I knew Miriam as a young girl, she went to school with my Beattie so I knew her mother died, leaving two young girls. I felt so bad for them, a tragedy.

When I was talking with Anne, I suggested Phil should meet Miriam's sister, Jeanne. I was afraid he would be a bachelor forever. He never wanted to look at girls or get married. Anne introduced them, they got acquainted and went together for a while. I said to Phil, 'Why waste time? What are you waiting for? Get married, you're 25 already.' At that time 25 was an old man. Then it got serious. Jeanne had the best life with Phil. She couldn't wish it any better. Always helping Phil. Always from the beginning. She saw anything had to be done, she did it. Your mother was a princess—a good soul. She should only rest there and wait for her children.

A night out with the family (circa 1946)

Like so many photos marking so many family occasions, this one has no inscription to specify people, place or event. But my eye goes to the three young couples—Sophie's three children and their spouses. They form a triangular constellation around Sophie and Abe—Phil and Jeanne to the left, Milton and Anne back-centre, Bea and Herman to the right. Our mothers stand out in their stylish black suits, sporting stylish chapeaux: Jeanne in a white straw boater, Anne in a black Parisian felt and Bea in a flower-strewn wide brim.

As always Sophie sits in the centre, pivot point of this melange of children/siblings/nieces/nephews. The vitality of her position is striking, her blouse blazoning the embroidered letters *S K P*—Sophie Kamler Pinker. Abe sits beside her, her constant. Perhaps it is their anniversary, a carnation pinned to his lapel, a corsage at her shoulder, above her heart. In the years to come, Sophie will wear the corsage at so many family occasions—full-bodied, pink-centred, flowering—emblematic of her matriarchal might. Yet here Bea also wears the corsage, we can only wonder why.

Milton marries Anne (1937)

Milton was besotted with Anne from the moment they met. She was attractive, slim, always careful with her dress—even as a child she wore white gloves to the local candy shop. Her father Edward Greenbaum was a furrier who settled the family in Ann Arbor, Michigan, a highly regarded university town. In the years to come, three of Anne's children would attend the University of Michigan, but she only finished her first year of study, as Milton took her to New Jersey after he graduated. Hurtled from the mid-west to east-coast Jewish culture and Sophie's orbit, I imagine Anne felt quite at sea. Often on Sunday visits to Sophie, she excused herself with a bad headache.

Like many wives and mothers of the '50s and '60s, Anne worked hard to sustain her husband and four children. I remember her as serious, quiet, contained. But her children remember the pleasure of laughing with her, an aspect many of us never witnessed. It was always Milton who took centre stage— a gregarious storyteller, sharing jokes, smoking a cigar in his armchair. Like my mother, Anne was the conciliatory partner who made the peace and began working outside the home (as receptionist in Milton's dental practice) after her youngest began high school. Following Milton's death in 1999, Anne moved to California closer to children Gloria and Howard, and found new energy in a retirement community where she lived another 14 years, until she died, aged 98.

Bea marries Herman (1938)

After Bea married Herman she moved with him to Tuckerton, New Jersey, where his family was well established. He was the only one of four siblings to graduate from university. Herman began at Harvard, but when the Depression hit and the family had inadequate funds for tuition, he completed his law studies in Newark. As the only lawyer in town, Herman was highly respected—serving on boards, negotiating contracts, wills, real estate closings and mediating countless local disputes in his living room, like a revered judge. He became a legend in town when he and a small group of businessmen opened a local bank mid-1950s. Herman handled all the legal work—and in the early 1970s his son Alan joined him to expand their legal practice.

Yet if anyone were to look in on our extended family gatherings, they would never guess at the elevated standing of this man. We knew Herman as modest, quiet, compliant. And he never took the limelight—he left that to Bea. But there was a moment—a Passover at Milton's house, when he startled us.

After dinner, as Bea played the piano and we sang along, Herman rose from his chair and belted out a Louis Armstrong version of *Hello Dolly*. Word perfect, vibrato, arms-wide-open—as if he'd been practicing for years. We whooped and cheered his extraordinary performance, never to be repeated. Just a glimmer of the lively fellow who stood so tall outside his home. Herman died in 1982 after a heart attack, aged 73, as quietly dignified as he lived.

Phil marries Jeanne (1944)

My mother, Jeanne, said happiness began when she married our father, Phil. He was seven years older, handsome, worldly; she was beautiful, funny, naive. Her early years were marked by upheaval and terrible loss. Her father, Morris Heidenreich, a German-born immigrant, was a gambler and aspiring entrepreneur who moved the family often, from Houston to Yonkers to the Bronx to

Chicago to Newark, and then Jersey City. Her mother, Sybilla, died suddenly at age 45, after an incompetent surgeon removed a tumour of such dimensions she believed herself to be pregnant.

I sometimes imagine our mother's loneliness as an exceptionally smart student, (advanced three school years ahead of her peers), without her mother. Yet there was always a lightness to Jeanne's spirit, an optimism, perhaps because of all she survived. She was big-hearted, short-tempered, forgiving and always fond of euphemisms. *Don't cry over spilt milk. A stitch in time saves nine. Beauty lies in the eye of the beholder.* She married a man who was *not easy*, but always found ways to keep harmony.

She never revisited the past with complaint, and lived more in the present than I've ever managed in my life. Housework could always wait. A voracious reader, admired for completing the *New York Times* Sunday Crossword in one day, she later became an able businesswoman, joining our father in the bicycle business in 1965, after my sister began high school. When Jeanne died of cancer in 1982, aged just 58, we reeled for years without her—our keystone gone.

Til death do us part

Sophie's children all had long marriages until death intervened. Daughter-in-law Jeanne was the youngest to die at 58; son-in-law Herman five months later, at

73 and son Milton, at 86. Only my father sought other partnerships, remarrying and divorcing later in life. It's clear to me, however, that Sophie disapproved of divorce. When I asked why her parents never dissolved their marriage, given their long separation and her mother's misery when they reunited in New York, she gave me that look— searing, disapproving.

Nothing like that. No. They were just mad at each other, that's all. My father wanted to stay in London, Mama insisted to return to Plonsk. They were just mad.

I find the idea of being *mad* an enigma, given that Rachael and Jacob were never suited and fought continuously. Rachael stayed in that marriage until all nine of her children married. When she finally left Jacob, she set up a small business selling pine nuts and peanuts from a cart on the streets of lower Manhattan and became financially independent. A de facto divorce, in my eyes, but not part of Sophie's worldview. Too modern a concept, perhaps. I'm not sure what she thought about three of her grandchildren divorcing. Marriage was for life—you suffered, you coped, no matter what.

That was not my stance. My first marriage lasted 14 years, but there were many warnings I failed to heed. Most notably in 1974, when the banks of the Murrumbidgee River broke, drowning our modest weatherboard home in Wagga Wagga, New South Wales. Water covered the land and surrounding acres were swamped by hordes of crickets and frogs roaring at night. The aftermath a nightmare—silt seeping through cupboard cracks, carpets soaked, bulging walls leaving mildew, fungus and rot. The smell impossible, the footings undone and me holding tight to a marriage too wrecked to right. Ten years later we divorced. I should have read the signs.

VII Sorrow

In memoriam (circa 1948)

IN MEMORIAM

ABRAHAM KAMLER

ON October 19, 1948, Mr. Abraham Kamler, a well known figure in bicycle circles in the State of New Jersey for the past 30 year, passed away at the age of 59.

Mr. Kamler conducted a bicycle business in Newark and was one of the larger dealers in the State of New Jersey.

His entire life was devoted to the bicycle field from the time he first immigrated to this country in 1906. He began work in a bicycle shop in New York and from his savings began a small business in New York City. In 1919 he purchased his bicycle business in Newark which he operated under the name of Kamler's Cyclery, up to the time of his death.

He will be missed by the many friends and dealers alike, who looked to him for advice and guidance in the conduct of their business.

There is something comforting about written proof—the obituary, census, marriage certificate—records that say I existed, I was here in my time with all my achievements and imperfections. The written record lies beyond memory, beyond the story told, the photo kept. Most of Abe's grandchildren only knew him by such documents, old love letters sent across time, a glimpse of a man well-loved and well-respected.

Abe's death

Most of us were not alive when Pop died in 1948, or were too young to remember. But Jay, his eldest surviving grandchild, remembers. Pop was always sick, always coughing, he recalls. The summer of 1945, when Bea took Jay to the Catskills with Abe and Sophie, was particularly upsetting. They stayed in one of the modest bungalow colonies often frequented by Jewish families, called a *kachalayn*. *Kachalayn* means eating in. Their small dwelling was private, but they ate communally in a huge kitchen. At least 10 stoves and 10 kitchen tables were spread around the periphery, with each family allocated their own space so they could eat *in*, not *out*.

But one evening Pop had a racking coughing attack that wouldn't stop until they finally called in the house doctor. This was years before his death from congestive heart failure, but a precursor to years of failed operations and ill health. No stents, no transplants, no bypass surgery back then, or he might have lived longer.

Pop's death at age 59 was traumatic for eight-year-old Jay. 'My father took me out of school in Tuckerton that day; I couldn't possibly grasp what death meant. I kept asking questions on the long drive to Newark which my father couldn't answer. Why did he die? How did he die? What happens when you die?'

When they finally reached Nana's apartment, Jay witnessed Sophie completely out of her mind with grief—keening, wailing, howling—surrounded by her friends. When she fainted, they dispensed smelling salts. Jay found it terrifying to see a woman of such strength out of control, collapsed on the floor. 'I didn't know what I was supposed to do or say? I said, "Hello Nana," and she howled even louder, holding me tight. I know my mother promised Abe she'd take care of Sophie after he died. And she lived that promise the rest of her life.'

Sophie marries Izzy (circa 1957)

Sophie and Izzy married in April 1957, nine years after Abe passed. I am struck by how serious the bride and groom look as they walk down the aisle, festooned with ribbons and vases of white orchids. Sophie wears pearls and white gloves, Izzy bow tie and tuxedo. They

are beautifully dressed, but there is no evocation of a joyous occasion. Yet the solidity of their bodies speak of their bond, a decision to move forward together as a unit.

Where or how Sophie met Izzy Landau is a matter for speculation. He was a kind man, short and squat, same height as Nana. He worked as a butcher, perhaps they connected during her weekly shopping. Or perhaps a mutual friend introduced them. No one is sure. But we do know he owned a small deli and brought home cold cuts and rolls in a small paper bag.

We know he was a good person, firm in his resolve to stand by Sophie, and like Abe in many ways—quiet, decent, affable, happy to do whatever Sophie wanted. He was her devoted driver, for errands and outings, wherever and whatever she needed. We called him 'Grandpa Izzy' and vividly remember him driving his big Chevrolet. His short neck was never visible, his bald head barely peeking over the steering wheel.

In 1961 they travelled to Israel on a cruise, perhaps a belated honeymoon, and the first time Sophie set foot on a boat since her arrival in America, some 50 years before. Later she reminisced with great emotion about the trial of Adoloph Eichmann in Jerusalem, televised during the time she stayed there.

Sadly, the marriage did not last long. Izzy's death six or seven years later marked a new sorrow and a significant transition for Sophie. She sold the Ivy Hill apartment in Newark and moved to South Jersey, to the Mayfair Apartments on the boardwalk in Atlantic City, closer to daughter Bea and her family.

VIII Siblings

Celebrating together (circa 1962)

We know so little about Sophie's eight siblings—just scraps of information, one-liners. Frank peddled three-ring bagel pretzels from his cart on the streets of lower Manhattan. Morris sang in amateur theatre, but was always sickly and died early. Ida had emotional problems and married Sam Neblekoff, surname later changed to Knobel. Hymie and Louis, the twins, were Sophie's baby brothers by 16 years. Annie was Sophie's closest sister. She married Harry, a tough guy with a gun and a warm heart, the man who took over the bike shop from Abe and Sophie when they left New York.

The photo captures Sophie, Annie and Harry in a moment of merriment at Jay's wedding in 1962. Spirits are high as Harry, far right, raises his glass in a toast—perhaps he's leading the group in song? The women are dressed for the occasion in silk, lace or brocade knee-length cocktail dresses, pointy-toed silk pumps and bouffant hairdos in the style of the times. The men in dinner suits or tuxedos.

Proud grandmother Sophie seems relaxed, standing far left, near her favourite sister Annie, close companion throughout her life. Unlike most family photos which place Sophie ceremoniously at the centre, husband by her side, here she stands behind Izzy. My eye is drawn to her right hand, looped around her husband in an affectionate hug, a surprising gesture never witnessed by any of her grandchildren.

While this is Jay's wedding day, the smiling groom and his bride Deanna, with back to the camera, are engaged in other conversation and not central to this boisterous montage. Rather it is Bea, mother of the groom, who takes centre stage. Beside her are Annie's two daughters, Sylvia and Katie, smiling broadly—

flanked on either side of Natchie, Sylvia's husband. There are few photos in the Sophie archive that exude such unguarded joy.

Where's Louis? (circa 1950)

Sophie's twin brothers, Hymie and Louis, were always spoken of in the hyphenated phrase, 'Hymie-and-Louis', their names as inseparable as the placenta they shared at birth. They were only five when Sophie brought the family to America. As a young man Hymie married Lilly (that marriage stuck), and Louis married Marie (that marriage did not). Everyone loved Louis; he was the funny one, lively, a joker.

But one day he vanished. Left the family, left the state, nowhere to be found. At first, his wife had no idea where he went, nor did his two kids. Bea's son Jay really missed him. 'Where's Louis?', he would ask again and again. 'Where's Louis?' He received no answer from the adults.

Perhaps they knew Louis fled to California. Or that he found work as a short order cook at Nate 'n' Al's Deli, an institution in Los Angeles. Or that he was gay. But if they did know, they didn't say. Gay sexuality was a shameful secret in the '50s. Our family did not speak of such things. Or of marital discord. Or mental illness. Or so many other taboo topics. And certainly no one told Jay about Louis.

Beach lovers (circa 1946)

Here they stand, Sophie and Abe at Miami Beach, Florida, feet planted in the sand, arms around each other. No hint of the glam-gloss beach scenes paraded today on Instagram posts or in magazines. Bathing suits are baggy and to the knee; bodies are tanned, not revealed—not sleek, not smoothed. Yet this is the American Dream come true for poor immigrants from Poland. Idyllic time and space to sunbake and schmooze with family and friends, as Sophie does in this vibrant tableau—her hands resting on the shoulders of Annie and a woman who is unknowable to us now.

Sophie also loved the beaches on the Jersey shore, an easy drive from Newark and the suburbs where her offspring settled. Every summer Milton and Ann rented a house at Beach Haven—their kids loved the sand and surf and attending local musicals at the Surflight Theatre. Bea and Herman's homes in Atlantic City and Margate were always proximate to the ocean and walking along the boardwalk.

But Florida also beckoned, as it did for many Jewish families fleeing freezing northern temperatures. For years my father Phil trekked us to Miami by car, an exhausting 24-hour drive through the night, with multiple candy and petrol stops. As a widow, Sophie continued to travel to Miami with Bea, by train (the Silver Star out of Philadelphia), but modestly. She preferred small kosher hotels to the showy palaces on Collins Avenue, like the Fontainebleau, and relished performances at the Yiddish Theatre.

Later in life, her children morphed into snowbirds, migrating south over winter. On retiring, Milton and Ann settled permanently at Pembroke Pines. Herman purchased condominiums at Hollywood and later Pompano Beach. Phil rotated through a series of homes in Hallandale, Boca Raton and Palm Beach—departing New Jersey after Thanksgiving, and returning in April for spring.

My father seemed kinder in southern climes, less tense, more jovial. Perhaps they all did. But it does seem the beach gene was passed on from generation to generation. As fate would have it, Sophie spent her last years at Seashore Gardens, a nursing home in Atlantic City, with good views of the sea.

Louis speaks back

When I travelled to Atlantic City to speak with Sophie in 1982, Louis was staying at Bea's house. He had no home of his own by then and rotated between the homes of his nieces. He seemed a relaxed man at age 76, tanned and in good health with a gold necklace peeking out from his shirt collar. As he came into the room, he asked, 'You done talking yet?' and settled into a chair to join us.

At first, Sophie seemed to welcome his entry, especially as he underlined her significance in the family. 'Everyone came to Sophie' he said. 'We all looked up to her. She was the main help—like a mother to us. She's the one who brought us to America. She's the one. Only her.'

It still surprises me that I never understood the import of Sophie rescuing her mother and seven siblings until that day. Steerage class tickets for one adult and seven child passengers, all purchased by Sophie. At the turn of the century these tickets cost US $25–35. Not expensive by today's standards, but impossible for those living in poverty in Eastern Europe. Not surprisingly, many immigrants relied on prepaid tickets sent by relatives already in America. How many years did it take Sophie to raise the funds? What were the difficulties? Did she always understand it had to be her? Noone said. But Louis knew.

He was keen to show me photos of his children and grandchildren that afternoon, but this clearly upset Sophie.

He doesn't see those kids, doesn't know what happened to them. Tell her.

Then with a sharp tongue she cut him down—the way she could slice skin with serrated syllables.

You still with that fat man? You still see him? What did you do with that jerk? That Nazi.

Louis ignored the slash and I watched in awe as he stemmed the flow of blood. 'No', he said, 'the man was not a Nazi, he was German, actually Bavarian. And no, we're not together, but still friends. I met up with him in California last year, for old times' sake. He took me to Germany once,' Louis elaborated pointedly, 'and I met his family. For your information, they live just as nicely as we do here in America.'

I observed Sophie pull back her sword. She was by this time reliant on Louis's good will and generosity. He often stayed at Bea's home in Margate—and was currently ensconced as the primary support system for his big sister and niece. He shopped and cooked and cleaned for them, provided transport to medical appointments, pharmacy and social events, as had Grandpa Izzy before him.

Later, after Nana moved to Atlantic City, it was grandson Alan who took over. He shopped for her, paid her bills and completed her legal paper work. He picked her up for dinner and, on occasion, drove her as far as Bradley Beach, some 75 miles (120 kilometres) away, to meet her sister Annie for weekends at the beach. For Alan these acts of service were a given; he indicated no sense of being imposed upon. Sophie needed help, Izzy was gone, it was his turn. Fact. And yet Sophie always had the knack of corralling the men in her life to pay heed to her every need, and serve her willingly.

IX Grandchildren

Mother's Day Lunch (circa 1959)

Here we are celebrating Mother's Day at a local restaurant. Sophie is the matriarch of this tribe, seated at the head of the table beside Izzy and as always, daughter Bea. All heads are turned towards the camera, smiling. There is an air of formality to the occasion: men in suits and ties, women coiffed at the hairdresser, children told to 'dress nicely' for Nana. Even the little boys wear bow ties.

Seven of Sophie's nine grandchildren are assembled for this occasion. It is one of the only images we have retained of us together. On the far side beside Izzy sits Howard, Milton's son. The youngest girls, Linda and Gloria (ages 6 and 7) sit together, lodged between their parents. On the opposite side Alan and Arnold (age 10 and 9) looking cheeky, and then Susie and me (age 13 and 12). We often paired off in this manner, across the family constellation—the little girls, the chubby boys, the older girls. Missing here are Sophie's two eldest, Jay and Lynn, most likely away at university.

Sophie's children and their spouses look particularly relaxed: to Sophie's left, Bea and Herman; mid-table opposite side, Milton and Ann, and at the far end, Phil and Jeanne. In so many photos over so many years this is the pecking order: first Bea, then Milton, then Phil. Looking back, it seems an obvious blueprint given the mother-sibling dynamics, but not necessarily visible to those present on the day. If any discord lies beneath the surface, it is well-guarded.

Gefilted

Nana was not a hugger, but at every birthday and bar mitzvah, every Passover and Thanksgiving, she was present. On Sunday visits she baked *kichlich*—crunchy pastry bow ties, heavily coated with sugar—or *rugelach*, crescent-shaped pastries originating in the Jewish communities of Poland, wrapped around a rich chocolate filling. The green glass dish on her coffee table, always spilled out half-moon jelly slices, rows of orange yellow and green, lightly sprinkled with sugar. We loved them.

Feeding was Nana's medium of affection. To refuse her food was to refuse love, almost impossible. She cooked the traditional Polish way, from scratch. Her gefilte fish with fiery horseradish was the stuff of legend. (*Gefilte* means stuffed in Yiddish.) Two days' labour for Nana. Buy the fish and let them swim in the bathtub overnight. Boil and debone the carp, pike and mullet. Ignore the unspeakable odour spoiling the kitchen. Mince the fish into patties with eggs and breadcrumbs, boil them in a simmering fish stock and place a slice of carrot on top. I'm not certain I liked gefilte fish as a child, but later it spoke of comfort, old Europe, the pogroms Nana fled, and survived.

It was my American-born mother who devised the gefilte shortcut. Jeanne was a woman of her time—under no circumstances would she spend days in her kitchen when a convenient alternative was available. Her approach was to purchase jars of Mother's Gefilte Fish, with the orange label, and empty the contents into a large pot of boiling water, heavily laden with sugar. She peeled carrots and simmered the broth until the very salty fish balls (preferred by Germans) became sweet, Polish-style. Convenient, fast, just right—a recipe many in the family emulated. Today I buy mine ready-made from the Balaclava Deli on Carlisle Street, St Kilda because they evoke home. Although prepared over 10,000 miles away from the kitchen where Nana laboured, they taste *just* like hers.

Remembering Nana

Howard remembers a large jar of schmaltz on Nana's kitchen bench, just near the sink. Yellow layers of rendered chicken fat were cooked down from chicken skin until it became a golden liquid. When cooled the liquid schmaltz solidified like butter. Some claim it adds a buttery richness to roast potatoes, chopped liver and matzah balls, but its reputation as a 'death food' prevails, guaranteed to clog the arteries of any pulsating heart. *We've got to give you some schmaltz*, Nana would say to Howard, as she spread it thickly on his bread. *You're too skinny, you're gonna' get sick. Look at your bones. You need to eat.* It was her way of loving.

Jay remembers living with Nana in 1949, the year his mother took him out of school in Tuckerton to reside in the Irvington apartment. Every night Nana cooked dinner because, Jay says, 'My mother was a terrible cook. I loved her crispy potato pancakes and tender beef flanken in soup broth. Nana loved to feed me. No surprise, I grew to be a fat kid.' During the polio epidemic, he recalls Nana hung a string of garlic around his neck to ward off germs and disease. But the time that shines most brightly was a Saturday afternoon matinee at a Roy Rogers movie. Sophie agreed to take Jay, amidst hordes of screaming children throwing popcorn and small boys firing off their cap guns. Amazingly, she endured 60 long minutes as the King of Cowboys and his faithful horse Trigger paraded their heroics. Whenever a cowboy was shot or fell precipitously from his horse she cried out, *Oy Oy Oy.* But Jay says she never complained.

Linda remembers a weekend with Nana at Bradley Beach, on the Jersey Shore, when she was five. Nana had rented a room in a boarding house close to the ocean. On the drive there, they pulled off the Garden State Parkway for a picnic lunch of Nana's meatloaf sandwiches on white bread. 'They were disgusting', Linda recalls, 'the cold congealed meat made me ill.' To be fair, she was a child who hated to eat, especially meat. Next mishap was a splinter in her foot from walking barefoot on the boardwalk. Nana took the crying Linda back to the house for repair. 'And she pushed a million grapes into my mouth. It'll be OK, she kept saying as she popped grape after grape in my mouth. By the time I stopped choking the splinter was out. Her tactic worked, but I've not eaten a grape since.'

Sue remembers the day Nana taught her to make stuffed cabbage. First, they prepared the chopped meat with onions and rice. Then, cored the cabbage and placed it in boiling water so the leaves gently unfolded. Finally, they rolled the meat-filled cabbage parcels with care, lest they break. Each step deftly done, quiet, methodical. They steeped the rolls in a rich sauce made from tomato paste and tomato soup, adding lemon juice, raisins, salt and sugar. So sweet. And sour. Nana's way of creating something from nothing, a way to reach out to Milton's daughter.

Alan remembers Yom Kippur 1983, when he and then-girlfriend Barbara drove Nana to synagogue on this most solemn of Jewish holidays. A time for reflection, forgiveness and fasting. The service had already begun when they arrived, but Sophie insisted on moving to the front to sit near her friends. She walked slowly with her cane and stopped suddenly mid-aisle to rest. Turning to Barbara she shouted, *When are you going to marry my Alan?* Deeply embarrassed, Barbara whispered, 'When he asks me.' Then she swung her cane at Alan—and in a loud voice, *It's time to get married Alan. It's time!* Oblivious to social graces or who she might disturb on this holiest of evenings, Nana had her say and moved to her seat. The couple were engaged shortly after.

Cousin COVID gathering

While the COVID pandemic separated loved ones precipitously, my cousins and I found a peculiar long-distance closeness as we met monthly on Zoom in 2020. Scattered across cities, states and countries, we rarely gathered face to face as adults, or if so, sporadically. But Zoom made contact easy, once we sorted the time differences between New Jersey, Vermont, Florida, California and Australia.

I'm not certain who suggested we meet, but all eight of us were keen. Sophie had nine grandchildren but Milton's eldest daughter, Lynn, died cruelly from a brain tumour, at 66. We are now the eldest of Sophie's descendants, ranging in age from Phil's youngest, age 71, to Bea's eldest, 84. Our parents passed away long ago.

Jay took the emcee role, inviting us in turn to share news of family, navigating lockdown in our disparate communities, and how our ageing bodies were holding up (or not). All of us, we learned, were COVID-cautious, committed to masks and vaccinations. The recitation of collective knee and hip surgeries, broken ankles, cataracts, heart and back problems, was received with empathy and humour. The talk enlivened us. We learned of Howard's sculpting and love of pickleball, Gloria's passion for her garden and lasting love with Alan, Jay and Ellen's idyllic retreat to Vermont leaving New York City behind, my brother Arnold's first grandchild, Sue's life in Florida, my sister Linda's recent artwork, Barbara and Alan's planned trip to the UK to meet their first grandchild.

I've wondered what Sophie might think of this brood? I know she disdained my living in Australia and disapproved of Gloria's move to an alternate community in California as a young woman. Yet we all married and collectively produced 17 great-grandchildren. Three of us divorced, but two remarried and found harmony the second time. And professionally, we achieved to Sophie's standard—two professors, two lawyers, one artist, one entrepreneur, one homemaker, one teacher/librarian, one health professional. Our contact has diminished since we've returned to life as usual—we meet every two or three months now, and not everyone comes. But our parents brought us together often as children, a bedrock for connecting at this more vulnerable time of our lives. I believe Sophie would have been pleased.

X Thanksgiving

101 North Frontenac (circa 1962)

Margate is a suburb of Atlantic City located on the Jersey shore, popular for its white sand beaches. This is where Bea and Herman moved in 1955 after they sold the unwieldy house in Atlantic City. 101 North Frontenac Avenue was a brand new, four-bedroom split-level home, stylish in its time. It is here Sophie's offspring gathered every Thanksgiving. In fact, a rotating holiday roster punctuated our year. At Passover we observed the first night seder at Phil's house, the second night seder at Milton's and Thanksgiving at Bea's.

Bea sticky-taped this photo to her mirror later in life—perhaps to reminisce or remember herself as a vibrant younger woman. For many of Sophie's grandchildren the house at 101 was a magnet, as was Aunt Bea—always welcoming and funny, a good storyteller. New York City was still her love, only 120 miles away, where she held a reserved seat at the Metropolitan Opera. Her house offered the perfect summer get-away—a free beach holiday and time away from our parents. Milton's youngest daughter Gloria spent several summers there, as did my brother who relished time away from our father's insistent gaze. We slept upstairs in the large recreation room, with guest beds and a large TV. Plenty of space and plenty of privacy. Bea filled the fridge with food from Casel's Deli and left us to our own devices.

At her home we felt free.

Arnold and Alan perform

Like most families across America, the fourth Thursday in November was a time for gathering and feasting. Late afternoon we sat together for a banquet of turkey, cranberry sauce, pineapple Jello mould, sweet potatoes and scrumptious pies—pecan, apple and pumpkin—all prepared by Hortense, the woman Bea hired for such occasions. Bea was never adept in her own kitchen.

It was after the table was cleared and chairs arranged in a semi-circle, that my brother Arnold and Bea's son Alan entertained us with their Annual Comedy Show—as pivotal to the day as the turkey. Alan, the main driver of the script, compiled jokes during the year from popular Jose Jimenez, Charlie Weaver and Allen and Rossi skits. The boys loved to tell jokes and loved the applause, but also created bit parts for the two youngest, Linda and Gloria. Each performance was taped—bad jokes, corny lines. It was a time of unrestrained fun capped off by a songfest at the piano, Bea pounding away on the keyboard. Now age 74, Arnold reflects:

'I thought Alan and I were quite talented and did a fantastic job. Many years later we found old tapes and listened together. I was shocked at how terrible we were—admirable but dreadful...better to have kept the memory alone. But actually no one cared, it was the event they loved.'

Announcer:	Since you enjoyed our first comedy skit, we're going to present another, this time on doctors. And now to the office of that famous general practitioner, Doctor Hackenbush.
Patient:	Is the Doctor in?
Nurse:	Yes, but the Doctor is practising.
Patient:	Well, I'll come back when he's perfect.
Doctor:	Nurse, bring in the next patient. Have you taken their temperature?
Nurse:	No, is it missing?
Patient:	Doctor you've got to help me.
Doctor:	What's the matter?
Patient:	I swallowed a roll of film.
Doctor:	Relax, I'm sure nothing will develop.
Patient:	Doctor, my brother is your next patient.
Doctor:	Call him immediately.
Patient:	I don't think he'll come if you call him immediately.
Doctor:	Why not?
Patient:	His name is Sam.
Patient:	Doctor, how much will this examination cost?
Doctor:	I'll examine you for $10

Patient:	Go ahead. If you find it, I'll give you half.
Doctor:	My how your heart beats.
Patient:	What did you expect it to do?
Doctor:	Stick out your tongue.
Patient:	What for? I'm not mad at you.
Doctor:	Have you ever been troubled with diptheria?
Patient:	Only when I try to spell it.
Doctor:	Oh dear, I think you're getting the measles.
Patient	(loudly) THE MEASLES!
Doctor:	Don't worry. I'll have you cured within a week.
Patient:	Now Doctor, no rash promises.

Pigeon poo

Early Thanksgiving morning our family and Milton's family made the annual two-and-a-half-hour car trek from North Jersey, along the Garden State Parkway, to Bea and Herman's home in Margate. When we sighted the water tower at the end of their street, we knew we'd arrived.

As was the custom, fathers and kids set off before dinner for a ritual walk along the boardwalk in Atlantic City, that famous promenade beside the ocean, memorialised by its own song. This was decades before the casinos and high-end hotels would dominate the landscape.

We walked, stopped for amusement games and rides on the Steel Pier (later closed in 1978) and indulged in what we now call junk food. To us, the delicacies were many. We loved the James Original Salt Water Taffy, a chewy, soft candy that oddly included no salt from the ocean; and we savoured their rich chocolate fudge. Hot peanuts in the shell from Planters Peanuts were also compulsory, as was Mr Peanut himself, the official mascot who greeted and lured potential buyers out the front.

But 1963 was a year we won't forget. November was cold, we were rugged up in coats, scarves and hats. As we arrived at Planters Peanuts my father, bald since his late 20s, removed his fedora hat—for just a moment to scratch his head. And at that exact moment, an errant pigeon dropped a large white glob of poo on his head. Splat! Oh, the look on his face as poo dripped from pate to cheek! The timing uncanny. All the kids went crazy with laughter. My father was a serious man, not a great smiler. I don't recall if he scowled or laughed with us. Perhaps we were too scared to laugh loudly, but certainly we snickered. Such a pleasure to witness this leveling of adult propriety, a moment of indignity when we glimpsed power…undone.

XI Endings

A hard life

I had a good life and a good husband, but a hard life. My children saw the way Abe and I lived together, like two children. I said it's night, so it's night. This is good, it's good. Never a word between me and Abe. Never. Only about the business partners we argued. He looked away; I couldn't take it. But I never thought in my life I would live to this age I am now. With my childhood, struggling to make a living, helping a husband. Why I have to suffer now, I don't deserve it. The kind of thanks I get? I can't take it. I don't wish it on nobody.

A failure of heart

We don't remember Nana being happy. With age, she became *cvetchy*, often steeped in complaint. Nothing was right. Her body ached from arthritis, she carried too much weight, her sons didn't visit. On one trip back to New Jersey I sat with her as she lay on her bed, eyelids watering unwanted tears. 'How are you feeling Nana?' She paused.

How should I feel? I wake up each morning, I'm still here. Enough already!

Her medical ailments were real. With Herman's passing in 1983 she became increasingly anxious and distressed. *I should have died*, she repeated over and over, *not him*. Her health deteriorated, walking became a challenge, she relied on a walker, then a wheelchair, and in time she could not sit up or get out of bed without assistance. As she lost mobility, plaque built up in her arteries. Hardening of the arteries they called it—arteriosclerosis.

Sophie believed it ran in the family. She was right. Bea endured high blood pressure most of her life and was panicked she might suffer an early death, like her father. Her remedy was to eschew salt and avoid exercise, although she lived a long life, until age 94. Milton had two heart attacks, the first at 60, which prompted retirement from dentistry and a move to Florida, for an easier lifestyle. But a second heart attack followed and then bypass surgery. He died of heart failure at age 86. Phil survived a quadruple bypass but died of a stroke four years later, also 86. I'm wondering: Can old disappointments narrow the arteries or create heartbreak? How curious it is that unlike Abe, his wife and three children lived long lives, even as their hearts hardened.

Shrinking spaces

The homes Nana inhabited trace the line of a journey from her itinerant beginnings as a newly arrived immigrant to her ascendance as matriarch, mother of three, grandmother of nine. In the early years she roamed between the homes of cousins/uncles/friends to escape her father. But after she brought her mother to America, she returned to the 'family' home on Pitt Street, which she described as a war zone. Marriage to Abe brought greater freedom, an apartment of her own, and a more comfortable life, especially after they moved to New Jersey.

The bicycle shop Abe purchased in Newark was located in the Weequahic area, a favoured location for recent Jewish immigrants, portrayed by Phillip Roth in several novels, most notably *American Pastoral*. My father was in the first graduating class of Weequahic High, also the alma mater of Roth in 1950, some 16 years later.

From the apartment at the back of Kamler's Cyclery in Newark, they moved to Irvington, only five miles up the road (eight kilometres), but signalling a rise in fortune into an emerging middle class. They bought the building at 545 South 21st Street—two apartments to each floor. They lived on the second floor, beside their good friends the Potters.

Sadly, Abe's death in 1948 marked the start of a gradual decline in space and horizon. Sophie bought a smaller apartment in a large complex called Ivy Hill Park, at 5

Manor Drive, Newark, never the most welcoming of places. The dark hallway was always redolent of days-old chicken soup, and her frightening neighbour, Mrs Felzenberg, always pinched my cheek when we visited, crying *shaina madel*, beautiful girl.

Sophie resided here alone for five or six years and then with second husband Izzy, until his death in 1964, when she moved again. This time from North to South Jersey, to the Mayfair Apartments in Atlantic City. Just 10 minutes from daughter Bea, she lived independently with the assistance of an aide named Jean. It was only after the building was scheduled to be torn down that she finally moved into Bea and Herman's home, inhabiting a bedroom at 101 North Frontenac. Full circle, back to the daughter who never left her side.

Ultimatum

Just as heart disease 'runs' in the family, so too might the ultimatum—the 'do as I say or else' syndrome. I call it a syndrome, cheekily, to signal a cross-generational disposition, more than an individual act of wilfulness. No discussion, no negotiation, no parsing a middle way.

Perhaps it began with Rachael Klemetz Pinker, Sophie's mother. When her husband Jacob moved the family to London, Rachael was unhappy. When she demanded they return to Poland after tolerating five years away, he refused absolutely. So, she returned to Płońsk without him and struggled to support their nine children on her own.

As a married woman, Sophie was no stranger to the ultimatum herself. She ruled her children firmly, even chasing them to school when they failed to drink their milk. When she insisted Abe relocate the family after the gangsters threatened their lives in New York, mild-mannered Abe found a property in New Jersey and began a new business. Later she pleaded with him to leave one business partner, then another, and another, because he did all the work—they did nothing; it had to stop. He never refused her.

My question is: how might such provocations seep into the consciousness of children? We know Sophie's children were so inclined. When Bea could no longer tolerate small-town Tuckerton, she insisted the family relocate to Atlantic City, later Margate. There she could find a Jewish community, the companionship of like-minded women and a more vibrant arts culture. Herman conceded and made the 30-mile commute to Tuckerton (quite rare back then) each day, until he retired.

My father, Sophie's youngest, also favoured the command. When I moved to Australia for two years but stayed on and on, despite his pleading, he felt betrayed and powerless. So, he did what the family knew best. It was too painful he said, me living on the other side of the world, coming home for visits, then leaving again. It had to stop. It was time for me to come home. And if I failed to return to America, he was done. He would never speak to me or my son again. When I did not return, he kept his word, holding his silence for seven years.

But as I view his edict now, peering through the wider family lens, I can see our pain from a different angle. Not just a clash of two individuals, but a collision that fits into an existent frame, like the last piece of a puzzle. Though I have carried that piece for as long I remember, biting, spitting invective, suddenly it finds a new context. It finds a space that was waiting for it—I hear an audible *CLICK* as it slots into place. A slight soothing, a sadness, a relief.

It is clear to me that the ultimatum never achieves predictable results. Never is it a given that the recipient will do as requested, or the issuer feel satisfied with the result. The imperative verb is merciless. It threatens, but leaves no space for give or take, for agency or grace. Once uttered, there is no turning back, no middle way. A ruthless desperation which ruptures every bond of affection. No one wins.

Seashore Gardens

Bea promised her mother, Sophie, she would *never* send her to a nursing home. But when she could no longer manage her mother's care at home, she did. Sophie lived the last two years of her life at Seashore Gardens Nursing Home, located on the boardwalk in Atlantic City. Sophie did not dislike the place. It was a Jewish facility with a good reputation. She was well cared for and knew some of the residents. She even participated in the program of concerts and speakers for a while.

Yet it seems Bea never visited her there. Grandson Alan and his wife Barbara lived close by and came often. As did Sophie's brother Louis, her niece Sylvia and from time to time, various grandchildren. Bea often spoke with her mother on the phone and sent Sophie's old carer Jean every day to check Sophie had everything she needed.

Given the depth of their companionship over a lifetime, it seems strange that Bea was absent the last years of her mother's life. Was she afraid to visit? Ravaged by guilt for breaking her promise? Or feeling too compromised to engage with Sophie face to face? We can only conjecture. Sophie died there on April 24, 1987, age 94.

XII Nana and Me

Leaning in to Sophie (circa 1956)

My entire life, indeed much of the time writing this book, I have remembered Nana as strong and unyielding, a powerful woman who was physically aloof. So, I am quite unsettled by this photo. Here we sit, I am leaning into her, as if it were always so. I am nine, my brother Arnold six and my sister Linda, three. They sit below at our feet, as in a separate montage, smiling broadly at our father, most certainly the photographer.

The image—an old polaroid photo—is deteriorating, much like my memory. But we are smiling, my head resting against Nana, her arm around me. She looks happy, uplifted, a youngish 63. Pearls grace her neckline. My arm reaches across to her. As I view us now, I feel held. Embraced.

But it is perplexing to find this photograph so late in this writing, when I have written our grandmother so large, so rarely tender. Is the image more reliable than memory? Or the absence of touch against skin? I don't know. But she is the family member I sought for solace and conversation after my mother died. She is the reason I boarded a Greyhound bus and travelled three hours to Atlantic City. She is the one I most wanted to sit with. Perhaps here lies the kernel of my passion to do Sophie justice, to let her memory sing in a family that does not make heroes.

Nana's breasts

Sometimes Nana liked company at night, before she married Izzy. I rarely slept at her apartment, but one Saturday night remains vivid. Her bedroom at Ivy Hill had two twin beds, separated by a bedside table with a frilly lamp. I was already tucked in, lamp light low when Nana entered to undress. She was a solid woman, short and stout. As she undressed, I tried not to look, but was mesmerised by the boned corset—cinching her waist, girding her breasts.

Barbara, help me unlace. Undo the knot at the top. Slowly I pulled the laces, uncertain how to proceed as I moved down her back, eyelet by eyelet, until she said, *Enough. I can finish.*

Nothing prepared me for the tumult of flesh. Two bell-shaped pendulums, long and heavy, falling downward past her waist. My mother had an ample bosom, but I'd never seen anything like this. I wasn't certain where to look, but when Nana turned her back to don her nightie I was lost in my pillow, embarrassed by the amplitude of her body. Somehow that revelation of womanhood was more than my 10-year-old self could handle. Yet now in my late 70s, I'm struck by the force required to keep Nana's body together, laced in tight.

Others before me have offered a feminist critique of the corset as instrument of torture, a patriarchal symbol of women's oppression, discomfort and subordination. But I wonder if this tough woman, once a lone-child traveller, donned the corset as armour, protecting her from harm, holding her tight and upright so she might keep going, no matter what. An exoskeleton, as strong as her will to survive, and stronger than the anguish buried inside.

Cry baby

The time I sat with Nana at her apartment in Atlantic City is crystallised—two figures perched on her balcony, overlooking the Atlantic Ocean. *I tell you Barbara, it's no good to live this long. Nobody should be so old.* This must have been 1976, she was 83 and I had been living in Australia four years. *Tell me, what's there for you in that place? So far away. No one should be so alone without family. Believe me Barbara, I know what I'm talking.*

All such conversation left me bewildered and speechless. It was not allowable in my family to say I liked or even preferred Australia. America was the only place to live, the place Sophie fled to as a young girl and which allowed her to forge a fortunate life. So, we sat in silence awhile, floating on the boundaries of time.

You were such a cry baby, do you remember? Crying every time we sat to eat. (I may have been a year old, maybe 18 months) *And your poor mother, never a night's peace. Only Abe could calm you, he knew how. Can you tell me why such a good man should die at 59? Can you tell me why?*

I have no answers for this woman, tired of living but still spitting syllables at me, without regard for their sting.

That last Friday night I'll never forget. You were hollering blue murder, Abe laying in the bed. 'Let me hold her,' he said. 'She'll stop crying, you'll see.' Sure enough, he staggered from the bed to his chair to take you in his arms. Such quiet. Such stillness until we finished the Shabbas meal. Two days later he died.

I take Nana's hand, ocean pounding below. Transported in time, feeling Papa close, I lay against his soon-to-be-stilled heart, yearning to have been loved much longer by this gentle, kind man.

Becoming Nana

When I became a grandmother at age 60, I worried about what I'd be called. I had no aspirations to be like Sophie then or adopt her no-nonsense, not-physically-affectionate manner. I aimed for the opposite and devoted every Tuesday to my son's two children—arriving at seven in the morning, when the parents left for work, and staying until I prepared dinner and ran baths.

The games we played together began unexpectedly. Picture us reading *Where the Wild Things Are*. When I reach the page where Max cries, 'Let the Wild Rumpus Start' I flap my arms, strum the baby ukelele and screech a crazy tune. Ruben and Lucy laugh and join in, roaring 'oooo oooo ooo yesh eeeh grhhhh' as we tumble to the floor—a moment of madness, no boundary, no adult looking on. As a working mother I entirely over-used the, 'not now, later darling' promise, always tired, always pushed for time. As a grandmother, time grew fluid, margins softened, everything was *now*, everything *yes*.

I am glad I decided to take Sophie's name, Nana. *Grandma* was too formal, *Nonna* not my culture. *Nanny* too Mary Poppins, *Granny* too old-fashioned. *Oma* too

German, *Bubbe* too Jewish. My grandchildren call me *Nana*. How I love the sound of it now. *Nana*. *Nana* can we? *Nana* will you? *Nana* where is? *Nana* what are we having for dinner? I took Sophie's name and came to embrace the memory of her voracious will, the reach of her arms, the tenderness beneath. I am proud to be Nana.

Cashmere sweater and pearls (circa 2023)

The white cashmere sweater has been sitting in my closet for the last 55 years. As I've moved from place to place, from one country to another, it has travelled with me. Now wrapped in plastic, slightly yellowed, the delicate silk lining is starting to perish, just as the memory of giving and receiving fades. The showy white mink collar, now a bit matted, was glamorous in its day. A gift from Sophie on my 16th birthday. Sweet 16, a coming-of-age garment for transitioning to adulthood.

It was Sophie's ritual gift to her granddaughters—to me, to eldest granddaughter, Lynn, and her sister Sue. Oddly, the two youngest granddaughters, did NOT receive the gift, much to my sister's disappointment. Why was that? Why did they miss out? Nana was 66 when I turned 16. Did she lose energy to sustain a family tradition she created? Or just forget? Another unanswerable question.

She also gave pearls when I turned 21—small white gems fastened by a gold heart clasp. They've kept their whiteness all these years, a sign of quality. I don't wear pearls, even as I appreciate their beauty. They feel too formal, too reserved. I am surprised when I see fashionable women don pearls with jeans on casual outings. Mine rest in a leather case in my top drawer—totem of a far-away time and the formidable woman who gifted them.

Recently I asked my 13-year-old granddaughter to try on the sweater and pearls. The ensemble seemed a strange costume to her—old-fashioned, disconnected from any past she knew or understood. She put them on to please me. And I snapped the photograph. But see how the cashmere hugs her narrow waist and long slender arms, reaching across generations—to Nana and to me.

General References

Alroey, G. (2007). Out of the Shtetl. In the footsteps of Eastern European Jewish emigrants to America, 1900 – 1914. Leidschrift: Organisatie En Regulering Van Migratie In De Nieuwe Tijd. 22(April), 91–122. https://hdl.handle.net/1887/73038

Barthes, R. (1993). *Camera Lucida: Reflections on Photography*. Random House, Vintage Classics.

Hirsch, M. (1997). *Family Frame: Photography, Narrative and Postmemory*. Harvard University Press.

Klier, J. (2010). Pogroms. *The Yivo Encyclopedia of Jews in Eastern Europe*. Vivo Institute for Jewish Research. https://yivoencyclopedia.org/article.aspx/Pogroms

Library of Congress. (2018). *Immigration and Relocation in U.S. History*. Polish/Russian, A People at Risk. https://www.loc.gov/classroom-materials/immigration/polish-russian/a-people-at-risk/

Library of Congress. (2018). *Immigration and Relocation in U.S. History*. The Lower East Side. https://www.loc.gov/classroom-materials/immigration/polish-russian/the-lower-east-side/

Malcolm, J. (2023). *Still Pictures: On Photography and Memory.* Text Publishing.

Mintz, S., McNeil, S. (2018). *Immigration Restriction. Digital History.* https://www.digitalhistory.uh.edu/disp_textbook.cfm?smtID=2&psid=3295

Płońsk Memorial House. (2023). *The idea behind the creation of the Memorial House.* https://dompamieciplonsk.pl/en/about-us/

Szymańska, O. (n.d.). *Jews in Płońsk.* The Emanuel Ringelblum Jewish Historical Institute. https://www.jhi.pl/en/articles/jews-in-plonsk,141.

Yadvashem (2024). *The Story of Płońsk:* A Jewish Community in Warsaw Province, Poland. https://www.yadvashem.org/yv/en/exhibitions/communities/plonsk/index.asp

Acknowledgements

In the end there is a book. Along the way there are critical conversations that allow the book to emerge and shine. I am indebted to those who probed Sophie Kamler's history with me and saw the possibilities; who filled in gaps and silences; who asked tough questions about structure, audience and legacy; who encouraged me to keep writing. This is the invisible and essential work that brings any book into being.

My heartfelt thanks go to many outstanding Australian writers for their stewardship. Long before I started writing, my treasured mentor and friend, Jordie Albiston, suggested my grandmother's story might best be written as collage. She was right. I have grieved her loss since she passed in 2022 and am grateful for all she taught me about poetic phrasing and form. Sian Prior's online *Advanced Creative Non-Fiction* course (2020) got me through months of COVID isolation. The vignette 'Nana's breasts' first took shape there. Sian's astute commentary made me believe I had more to say, as did gifted poet Mark Tredinnick in his online *Poetry Masterclass, What the Light Tells* (2022). There I found a voice to tell Sophie's story, and I am grateful for his insights as the narrative took shape.

Renowned poet Kevin Brophy has been a wonderful friend since 2008, when I departed the world of academic writing and enrolled in his poetry course at Melbourne

University. His generosity has been unstinting as he carefully read drafts, early and late, of *Sophie*. His questions, imaginings and gentle commentary helped me discover how to juxtapose photographs, family memories and stories of Sophie's *own* telling, so our mighty matriarch might live on the page, as in her life.

For their friendship and support, thank you to Marcia Jacobs, who translated Sophie's Yiddish to help me capture the lilt of her voice; to photographer Jodi Webb, for her sharp eye in sorting and editing the rich, but chaotic array of photos collected over many years; and to Sue and Tim Blashki, for exploring the complexities of writing about family. In the discomforting space of not knowing, and their quiet reassurance, I found my way.

My further thanks to Debbie Lee for saying, 'Yes!' wholeheartedly to publishing *Sophie*. Debbie became the new owner and publisher of Ginninderra Press in early 2024, following the retirement of the greatly admired Stephen Matthews, OAM. Her skilled team have shaped the final stages of the book with finesse. Thank you to Sarah Newton-John for her sensitive editorial work; and to Graham Davidson for his fine design, melding photos and text with care.

My deepest gratitude goes to my family—to my siblings Linda Levi and Arnold Kamler; to Bea's sons Jay and Alan Gerber, and Alan's wife Barbara Gerber; to Milton's children Howard Kamler, Gloria Kamler and

Sue Rubinfeld. Their candid memories of Sophie and her offspring greatly enrich this account.

Jay Gerber is the grandchild who knew Nana longest and best. I am especially grateful to him for his detailed stories and enthusiasm for the project; and to Barbara Gerber for her generous replies to my frequent questions. While Barbara married into the family, she lived closest to Bea and Sophie in South Jersey and became the unofficial archivist of family photos, for which we are grateful. Finally, I am thankful every day to my husband, Greg Levine, who inspires me to keep going and to write from the heart.

About the Author

Barbara Kamler was born in New Jersey and has lived in Australia for over five decades. She is a poet, memoirist and author of creative non-fiction, as well as eight academic books and numerous essays and chapters. *Leaving New Jersey* is a memoir of loss and reconnection told in prose poetry. *Love, Regardless*, a gallery of 14 long-love portraits, crafted into syllabic verse. In *Sophie*, Barbara creates a dynamic, multi-voiced collage of prose vignettes and photographs to tell the spirited story of her paternal grandmother, Sophie Kamler *nee* Pinker, who fled the pogroms of Poland at age 14, and ventured to New York City on her own. Barbara currently runs writing workshops for doctoral and early career researchers at a variety of universities in Melbourne, Sydney and Newcastle.